HOW TO COOK WILD GAME
first get the game

© Copyright 1993   G & R Publishing Co.

All rights reserved. No part of this publication may be reproduced in any manner without prior written permission of the publisher, G & R Publishing Co. Credit to publisher must be included in any excerpt.

Printed in the United States of America

ISBN 1-56383-021-3

TABLE OF CONTENTS

Ducks, Geese and Birds 1

Fish and Water Life 47

Small Game 89

Large Game 109

DUCKS, GEESE & BIRDS

Baked Coot (or Mud Hen)	35
Baked Ruffed Grouse	33
Beefsteak, Pigeon & Mushroom Pie	28
Broiled Canvasback Duck	4
Cleaning and Preparation of Wild Duck, Geese . and Upland Game	1
Duck A La Orange	8
Ducks Deluxe	10
Fried Pheasant	42
Fried Quail	25
Grouse	34
Grouse French Style	32
Hungarian Partridge	31
Long Island Duckling Cooked in Wine	13
Mourning Doves	26
Partridge	30
Pheasant with Apples	44
Quail	19
Quail in Wine	22
Quail Pie	23
Roast Duckling Hartford Style	12
Roast Goose with Sauerkraut Stuffing	14
Roast Mallard Duck	7
Roast Pheasant	43
Roast Prairie Chicken	40
Roast Quail German Style	20
Roast Squab	39
Roast Wild Turkey	46
Roast Woodcock	38
Smothered Pheasant	45
Smothered Quail	24
Snipe, German Style	36
Stewed Duck, French Marshall Style	6
Texas Quail	21
Wild Boiled Goose	15
Wild Duck	5
Wild Ducks, Geese and Pheasant	2
Wild Goose	17
Wild Pigeon	27
Wild Roast Goose	16
Wild Roast Goose, Canadian Style	18
Woodcock and Snipe	37

CLEANING AND PREPARATION OF WILD DUCKS, GEESE AND UPLAND GAME

Many old cookbooks and many old recipes on wild ducks and upland game were written long before the days of modern refrigeration. In spite of this, the advice they gave on the preservation of game was better than that of modern cookbooks which tell you not to wash out or soak out in salt water ducks, pheasants and other similar game. Clean well, draw and season your bird with salt and pepper, add a tablespoon of vinegar. Place in a cold water brine (about 2 tablespoons of salt to a quart of water) and allow to stand in a cold place overnight. Remove from the brine, dry thoroughly inside and out. Cold salt water tends to draw out the loose clotted blood particles and help to thoroughly clean your meat. It is very necessary because game that is killed with a shotgun does not have the same chance to bleed out as does domestic poultry that is killed in a butcher shop or in the back yard by whacking its head off with an axe.

WILD DUCKS, GEESE AND PHEASANT

There are a number of ways to prepare wild ducks and geese. Many fine mallard ducks are ruined through the selection of poor recipe or through the inability of the average hunter to distinguish the young duck or goose from the old. Naturally it takes long cooking for old birds and they can never be served rare or medium. One of the big problems in cooking wild geese is that it is impossible for the average person to tell their ages. History shows that there have been cases where Canadian geese have lived to be 70 years old. They frequently reach an age of 25 years. Naturally, these are not going to be very tender; on the other hand, you might get one that is only a year or two old. Some people prefer wild duck very well cooked. In that case, it is often desirable to parboil for ½ hour before placing in the roaster.

Young geese may be roasted, older ones will have to be stewed. They are prepared the same as wild ducks, although in the case of an old goose, it is best to skin it, as the skin adds an unpleasant flavor to the meat.

For those people who prefer duck with dressing, stuff with special game dressing. Halves of peeled apples make a very good stuffing. For those who prefer onion flavor, several peeled onions, cut in halves, may be substituted for a dressing. For those who prefer a well-done duck, it is preferable to put 1 quart of milk or consomme in the roaster and baste every 10 to 15 minutes with the hot milk. Roast duck well done should be roasted 2 to 3 hours in a moderate oven.

BROILED CANVASBACK DUCK

With a pair of game shears or a heavy sharp knife, remove the breast section of the duck. Rub thoroughly with salt and pepper and salt pork drippings. Boil under a 550° fire for 10 or 12 minutes. Baste with fat drippings so that it will not burn. Serve on a hot platter with drawn butter sauce mixed with the juice of ½ lemon and a little chopped parsley. Bring to table very hot in a covered dish if possible. Serve with fried bread crumbs and currant jelly.

WILD DUCK

5 Jonathan apples
Bacon strips
Ducks (2 mallards)
1 C. raisins
Salt and pepper
Spices

Season ducks with salt and pepper inside and out. Don't peel apples, quarter them, and place some apples and some raisins in each duck. Place ducks in roasting pan and put the rest of the apples and raisins around them. Add the spices which you favor. Place bacon strips on each duck. Pour about 1½ cups of water into the pan. Bake at 350° until tender. Add more water, if needed.

STEWED DUCK
(FRENCH MARSHAL STYLE)

1 pair fine ducks, French or
  canvasback
12 godiveau quenelles
12 mushrooms
2 onions, chopped fine
1 bay leaf
3 sprigs each of thyme
  and parsley

1 clove garlic
1 sq. inch of ham
1 T. vegetable oil
1 T. flour
Salt and pepper to taste
1 glass Madeira or sherry
  wine
Croutons to garnish

Prepare the duck exactly as in the recipe for "Stewed Wild Ducks". Add 10 minutes before serving 12 godiveau quenelles and the wine. Garnish the dish with croutons and 12 nicely cooked mushrooms. Cut in two. Send to the table hot.

ROAST MALLARD DUCK

Prepare duck in a cold water salt brine and allow to stand overnight. Remove ducks from the brine and dry thoroughly, inside and out. Salt and pepper inside, also add some celery salt, if available. Prepare quartered chunks of apples, onions and celery in about equal portions and fill the bird. Sew up and take thin strips of salt pork and tie around the breast of the bird. Put in a closed roaster, breast side down. Pour about 2" of water or consomme into the pan so the breast of the bird will be laying in the water. Place in an oven set at 350° and bake for about 3½ hours or until bird is tender. Take roaster from the oven and remove half of the remaining liquid. Turn the duck over so that it is now breast side up and put in a 400° oven for about 20 minutes or until the breast is nearly browned. Continue to keep salt pork on the breast. If it has melted away too much, put on fresh pieces. Baste occasionally while browning.

NOTE: An excellent way to cook ducks if you like them well-done and tender.

DUCK A LA ORANGE

1-4 to 5 lb. duckling
Salt
Pepper
2 cloves garlic, crushed
Pinch ground ginger

Pinch thyme
Pinch paprika
1 onion, sliced
1 stalk celery, chopped
1 carrot, sliced

Wash and dry duck. Rub inside and out with salt, pepper, garlic, ginger, paprika and thyme. Place onion, carrot and celery inside cavity. Place breast down on a rack in a roaster, cover and roast at 425° for 15 minutes.

Reduce heat to 350° and continue roasting 1½ to 1¾ hours, turning occasionally, ending with the breast side up the last 30 minutes. Remove fat from pan as necessary. Prick the duck skin with fork from time to time while roasting. Remove duck from roasting pan and keep warm. Drain off all but 4 tablespoons of duck juices from the roasting pan. To this, add 4 tablespoons flour and cook until flour is slightly browned. Add 2 cups chicken stock, ½ tablespoon Escoffier sauce, ¼ teaspoon Kitchen Bouquet and salt and pepper to taste. Melt ½ cup currant jelly with 4 tablespoons sugar in a saucepan. Add 1 bay leaf, a whole black peppercorn, ½ cup of the brown sauce from the stove, the juice of 2 oranges, the grated rind of 1 orange and the grated rind of ½ lemon. Boil for 10 minutes over a low flame. Add 1 cup more of the above brown sauce and boil. Strain sauce. Taste for seasoning and add ½ ounce Grand Marnier or Cointreau, if desired. Pour sauce over duck. Garnish with orange peel strips which have been parboiled in water and preserved kumquats.

DUCKS DELUXE

4 wild ducks
2 apples
1 large onion
4 celery stalks with tops
1 T. pickling spice
Cinnamon sticks

1 clove garlic (each duck)
1½ C. sherry wine or
  Burgundy
4 carrots
1 green pepper
2 oranges
Salt and pepper

Punch holes in skin of duck with ice pick and fry out excess fat. Cut vegetables and apples in large chunks. Add pickling spice. Stuff the well-cleaned ducks with this mixture. Coat the stuffed ducks with flour. Sprinkle top with powered cinnamon. Place on rack in baking pan and add enough chicken consomme or water to prevent burning. Tuck sliced oranges and cinnamon sticks around ducks. Cover and bake for 3 hours, basting occasionally. Remove top of baking pan and brown ducks for 30 to 40 minutes, basting about 3 times with the wine (might increase heat). When browned, remove ducks and pour fat off drippings in pan. Add flour to thicken and more water, if necessary, for gravy. Serve with wild rice.

ROAST DUCKLING
(HARTFORD STYLE)

1-4 to 5 lb. duckling
Salt
¼ C. mint jelly

¼ C. A.1. steak sauce
¼-6 oz. can frozen orange
juice concentrate*

Preheat oven to 350°. Rub inside of duckling lightly with salt. Place on rack in shallow baking pan, breast side up. Bake in moderate oven (350°) 2½ to 3 hours or until tender. Pierce surface of duckling with fork occasionally during roasting period. Meanwhile, combine mint jelly, A.1. sauce and orange juice concentrate in saucepan and cook over medium heat. About 30 minutes before duckling is tender, baste surface with some of the sauce. Heat remaining sauce to serving temperature and serve with duckling. (This sauce is equally good with lamb, pork or veal chops.) Makes about 4 servings.

*Substitute 1½ teaspoons grated orange rind, if desired.

LONG ISLAND DUCKLING COOKED IN WINE

1 duckling
2 medium-size onions
1 T. olive oil
1 sprig parsley
2 bay leaves
2 T. lard
1 pt. Claret, Burgundy, or
 dry red wine
1 jigger of brandy
½ lb. mushrooms

Preheat oven to 325°. Cut the duck apart similar to a chicken as for frying. Put the duck in an earthen crock and cover with the seasoning, mixed spices, onions, brandy and wine and let it stand for 3 or 4 hours. Put the oil and lard in a frying pan and brown each piece of duck. Remove each piece of duck from the frying pan and put into a casserole. Cover with the wine, etc., in which the duck has been soaked. Add the mushrooms and simmer in the closed casserole for an hour and 15 minutes at 325°. Serve in the casserole in which the duck is cooked and serve with it a salad and noodles with fried bread crumbs.

ROAST GOOSE WITH SAUERKRAUT STUFFING

1 goose, 12 to 16 lbs.
1 C. tomato sauce
2/3 C. sherry
4 pieces celery
2 large carrots, cut
3 C. water
3 T. salt

1/2 tsp. pepper
1 T. goose fat
1 large onion
2 lbs. sauerkraut
6 tsp. caraway seed
1 large potato, grated
1/2 C. water

Put carrot and celery into the bird and sprinkle salt and pepper into the inside. Put 3 cups water in the roaster, then the bird and then place in the oven for about 1 1/2 hours. Meanwhile, fry onion in fat. Add sauerkraut and grated potato and add caraway, salt, pepper, 1/2 cup water, sherry and tomato juice and mix your stuffing and let stand until you remove goose from oven. Turn bird every half hour in the oven. After 1 1/2 hours, take out of the oven, remove carrots and celery and replace with sauerkraut stuffing. Let the goose roast in a dry pan for another hour or more until well done. Baste occasionally with a little goose fat.

WILD BOILED GOOSE

Soak overnight in sweet milk. In the morning, wash and allow it to stand in cold water 1 hour. Fill the body with well-seasoned bread dressing, using salt, pepper, onions and sage. Tie up in a thin cheesecloth. Boil 2 hours. Serve with giblet sauce and gooseberry jam.

WILD ROAST GOOSE

Dress fowl 24 hours before using and soak in salt water 2 hours before cooking. Make a mashed potato dressing, seasoned with onion, vegetable oil, pepper and salt. Fill the body of the goose. Grease it all over well with vegetable oil and dredge with flour. Place in a pan with 1 pint of water. Baste well and cook 2 hours. Serve with onion gravy and applesauce.

WILD GOOSE

Clean and pick goose well. Do not skin. Lay the giblets to one side to use in the stuffing. Prepare stuffing as follows:

*2½ qts. stale bread,
  broken up
Goose giblets
1 large onion, chopped fine*

*2 Jonathan apples, diced
Salt and pepper
Sage
Garlic*

Boil giblets until tender. Remove skin and chop fine. Combine with bread, onions and apple. Mix well and add salt and pepper, sage, garlic and other seasonings to taste. Moisten and stuff goose. Place goose in roasting pan and spread with about 2 tablespoons of butter, and then sprinkle with a little flour. Roast in 350° oven until done, which will take about 15 to 20 minutes per pound. Baste often.

WILD ROAST GOOSE
(CANADIAN STYLE)

A roast goose is generally filled with sage-and-onion stuffing. The way in which this is made must depend upon the taste of those who have to eat it. If a strong flavor of onions is liked, the onions should be chopped raw. If this is not the case, they should be boiled in 1, 2, or 3 waters and mixed with a smaller or larger proportion of bread crumbs. It should be remembered, when bread crumbs are used, room should be allowed for swelling. Truss the goose firmly, tie the openings securely, put into the hot oven, and baste it plentifully until done enough. A goose is both unwholesome and unpalatable if insufficiently cooked. Take it up, remove the skewers and fastenings, pour a little gravy into it, and send some good gravy and either apple or tomato sauce to the table with it. Garnish with lemon. Time: 1½ to 2 hours.

QUAIL

Take a roasting pan, butter it liberally and melt the butter. Season the quail with salt and pepper and any other seasonings desired and place in the pan. Cover them with melted butter. Lay strips of bacon on each bird. Place in hot oven (475°) and bake for about 15 minutes. Reduce to moderate heat (350°) and bake until done. During the baking, be sure to baste often with the juices and butter. Can be served with gravy made from the juices or in any other way desired.

ROAST QUAIL
(GERMAN STYLE)

Draw the birds or not, according to taste. Truss them firmly and tie over the breasts a vine-leaf covered with a slice of fat bacon. Roast in a hot oven and baste well. When done enough, brush the bacon over the glaze and serve the birds on a hot dish. Garnish with watercress. Pour good brown gravy around, but not over the quails. Serve on toast. Time to roast the quails is 15 to 20 minutes. Sufficient, 2 for a dish.

TEXAS QUAIL

6 quail
¼ C. canned milk
1 C. flour
Salt and pepper
1 C. cooking oil
1 C. uncooked rice
2 C. water
1 can cream of mushroom soup, undiluted
1 can cream of celery soup, undiluted
1 medium bell pepper, chopped
1 C. chopped celery
1 medium onion, chopped
1 tsp. salt

Preheat oven to 350°. Dip quail in canned milk and then in seasoned flour. Brown in medium-hot cooking oil. Saute pepper, celery and onion in a small amount of butter. Mix uncooked rice, water, soups, sauteed vegetables and salt. Pour into buttered 9x9" casserole dish. Place browned quail on top of rice mixture. Cover and bake at 350° for 45 minutes or until rice is done. Serves 6.

QUAIL IN WINE

Rub 6 quail with a little salt and freshly crushed black pepper. Brown them lightly in melted butter and place them in a buttered casserole. To the skillet in which the birds were browned, add 1 carrot (diced), 1 small onion (chopped), 2 tablespoons chopped green pepper, ½ cup chopped mushrooms and 3 small slices of blanched orange peel. Cook the vegetables slowly for 5 minutes. Stir in 1 tablespoon flour, and add 1 cup chicken stock, gradually. Continue to stir until the sauce is thickened. Correct the seasoning with salt and pepper and simmer slowly for 10 minutes longer. While the sauce is cooking, pour ½ cup white wine over the quail and place the casserole in a moderate oven (350°) for 10 minutes. Pour the sauce over the birds, cover the casserole and cook for 20 minutes or until the birds are tender. Serve with watercress and currant jelly.

QUAIL PIE

Make a rich biscuit dough, using milk or cream for mixing. Roll thin. Spread with butter, fold and roll again. Line a baking pan with the dough. Split dressed quail down the back, lay them in the pan, sprinkle with salt and pepper, and spread each bird with butter. Add boiling water, about ⅔ cup to each bird. Cover with crust. Make some small slits to let out steam and bake in moderate oven until done.

SMOTHERED QUAIL

In skillet, brown four 4 to 6 ounce ready-to-cook quail, split in halves lengthwise, in ¼ cup butter. Season with salt and pepper. Top with ½ cup chopped onion. Add ½ cup light cream. Cover and simmer about 30 minutes or until tender. Remove quail to a warm platter. Blend 2 tablespoons cold water into 1 teaspoon cornstarch. Add to pan drippings. Simmer and stir until thickened and bubbly. Pour gravy over quail. Makes 4 servings.

FRIED QUAIL

Cut up quail as desired. (It is usually best to have 3 pieces - breast and 2 legs.) Season with salt and pepper and roll pieces in flour. Place in hot deep fat and brown quickly on both sides. Turn down heat and cover pan. Let cook slowly until tender. Make gravy right in the same skillet using residue left from frying.

MOURNING DOVES

Clean carefully. Soak out for 15 minutes in salt water. This bird is quite small and 2 or 3 birds are required per serving. Follow the same recipes as for quail. Also good in individual pot pies like chicken pot pie.

WILD PIGEON

Clean and salt young wild pigeons. Place in a crock or stone jar. Pour over them wine and vinegar. Add a sliced onion, several bay leaves, a few strips of lemon rind, and let it stand thus 2 days. When ready to cook, dry them with a cloth, interlard the breasts with strips of bacon, place in a roasting pan, dot with vegetable oil and roast, basting frequently with cream and the liqueur in which they have been pickled. Then brown vegetable oil and flour. Thin with the pickling liqueur. Add the liqueur in the roasting pan, sweet or sour cream and boil together until smooth.

BEEFSTEAK, PIGEON AND MUSHROOM PIE

2 pigeons
2 T. butter
1½ lbs. good stewing beef
2 pts. chicken stock
Salt and pepper

1-cup pkg. aspic jelly
¼ lb. flat mushrooms
Puff or flaky pastry made
   from 1 C. plain flour,
   1 egg, pinch of salt

Preheat oven to 425°. Cut meat in 1½ cm. squares (1"). Melt butter in saucepan, add pigeons, brown slowly. Remove and split in halves. Return pigeons, meat and stock to pan. Season with salt and pepper. Cover and cook slowly 2 to 2½ hours. Carve breasts from pigeons and discard carcass. Put meats and aspic into a bowl to cool. Quarter mushrooms and put in pie dish, add cooked meats and pie funnel. Cover with pastry and decorate. Glaze with egg, beaten well, pinch of salt. Bake at 425° for 20 to 25 minutes until pastry is ready. Serve hot or cold. Serves 4.

If necessary, fill baked pie through pie funnel with more stock and aspic. Good for shoots and fishing picnics.

PARTRIDGE

Partridge will need 40 minutes to cook, as the meat is white. It may be treated as chicken and cooked with or without dressing and is good either roasted or broiled. It is best served roasted without dressing, but should be garnished with a border of coarse bread crumbs which have been fried golden brown in hot vegetable oil. A white sauce or bread crumbs sauce should be served with it.

HUNGARIAN PARTRIDGE

Hungarian partridge originated in Old Austria-Hungary and here is a recipe used by the old Austrian-Hungarian cooks in preparing it. Partridges should be thoroughly cleaned and soaked out in strongly salted water to remove all clotted blood. Allow to soak out for several hours, changing the water several times, if necessary. A lardon or two of salt pork may be inserted in the breast and then also wrap several slices of salt pork around the breast. Melt some butter and into the melted butter, add some crushed juniper berries and use this for basting every 15 minutes. About 20 minutes before the birds are done, pour some sour cream over them and place the cover on the roasting pan and allow to steam with the sour cream. Skim off excess fat and make a pan gravy. Serve with grapefruit or Waldorf Salad.

GROUSE
(FRENCH STYLE)

Grouse is best roasted in a hot oven for 25 to 30 minutes. Inside each bird, put 1 tablespoon of vegetable oil and they should be basted frequently while cooking with vegetable oil or they may be cooked with strips of salt pork tied over the breast and thighs. A few minutes before serving, dredge them with flour, pepper and salt and serve with a brown gravy. The liver of the grouse should be boiled and pounded to a paste with butter, salt and pepper. Then spread on hot buttered toast with some of the juice from the baking pan. On these pieces of toast, the grouse should be served. Prairie chickens, pheasants and partridges are all cooked in the same way. If preferred, they should be split down the back, rubbed well with vegetable oil or butter, seasoned with pepper and salt and fried to a light brown. Then cover tightly and let steam over a small flame for 40 minutes. Make a gravy of the juices in the pan, blended with a little flour and 1½ cups of good rich stock.

BAKED RUFFED GROUSE

4 grouse breasts *1-10½ oz. can mushroom soup*

Preheat oven to 350°. Wash the grouse. Brown the grouse in a frying pan on the stove. Pour off the excess grease. Do not salt. Put grouse in a Dutch oven pan and add 1 can of mushroom soup. Cover with kettle and bake 1½ hours at 350°. If a person doesn't care very much for the mushroom flavor, then add ½ can mushroom soup and ½ can cream of chicken soup. The soup will help the grouse to remain moist. Serves 4.

GROUSE

2½ lbs. cleaned, cut-up
  grouse
1 C. sour cream
1 T. fresh lemon juice
1 tsp. salt
1 tsp. celery salt

½ tsp. ground black pepper
½ tsp. garlic powder
2 tsp. paprika
¾ C. flour
1 tsp. salt
⅓ C. shortening

Preheat oven to 400°. Place cut-up grouse in refrigerator dish. Combine next 7 ingredients and pour over grouse, being sure to cover all pieces. Cover dish and refrigerate overnight. Drain. Dredge in flour mixed with 1 teaspoon salt. Melt shortening in an 8x12" baking pan and place grouse in it. Bake in a preheated oven (approximately 400°) for 70 minutes or until done, turning to brown both sides.

BAKED COOT
(OR MUD HEN)

With a sharp knife, remove the breasts and legs only of a mud hen. Skin them out and soak in a strong solution of salt water for 4 or 5 hours. Remove and dry and place in a covered dish. Add salt and pepper to your birds and ½ bottle of good dry wine and 1 sliced onion and place in a covered dish in the refrigerator overnight. When ready for cooking, put the breasts and legs in a roasting pan. Brown the onions that were soaking in a little butter and add to the roasting pan. Also add ½ cup tomato sauce, salt and pepper, 1 cup consomme and bake in a preheated 350° oven for 1½ hours, being sure to turn each piece of mud hen every 15 minutes. Add 2 jiggers of sherry at the end of 45 minutes. Place in the oven again for about 30 minutes. By this time the bird should be well done and tender. Serve with wild rice and make a sauce of what is left in the roaster.

SNIPE
(GERMAN STYLE)

Pluck the birds, skin the head and remove the eyes. Singe them and cut off the claws. Twist the legs, disjointing them and bring the feet close to the thighs and put the long beak through these as a skewer. The position will indicate how the breast may be kept thrown up by passing twine around the joints and lower part of the body, to tie at the back. Put them in a stewpan just large enough to hold them, with vegetable oil, enough to keep them basted, turning as they are done on one side until they are tinged all over. About 20 minutes of a brisk heat will cook them. Toast slices of bread, pour on these the vegetable oil from the pan, and serve the birds on them. Dressed in this way, they are not drawn before the trussing.

WOODCOCK AND SNIPE

After wiping each bird carefully with a damp cloth, cut off the feet and skin the lower legs by dipping them in boiling water. Skin the head. Remove the eyes and twisting the head around, run the bill through the legs and body. This serves as a skewer to hold the bird in compact shape. Wrap each bird in a slice of pork or bacon and cook in a hot oven with vegetable oil, for 10 minutes. Boil the livers and pound them to a paste. Season with pepper, salt, butter and onion juice and spread on pieces of buttered toast, pouring the juices from the baking pan.

ROAST WOODCOCK

Pluck the woodcocks carefully, neck and head as well. Do not open them, but truss them securely. Roast in a hot oven, flour them and baste liberally with drippings of butter. Dish them with a piece of toast under each and garnish with watercress. Send melted butter or orange gravy to table in a tureen. It is an improvement to cover the woodcocks with slices of bacon before putting them down to the fire and when they are to be had, 2 or 3 vine leaves may be laid under the bacon. Time to roast the woodcocks if liked underdone, 15 to 20 minutes; if liked well done, 25 to 30 minutes. Sufficient, 2 for a dish.

ROAST SQUAB

Season 6 squab. Place a slice of salt pork over the breast of each, which can be kept in place with a couple of toothpicks. Place in the oven with 2 slices of carrots, 1 medium onion, 2 bay leaves, 6 peppercorns and a quarter of a pound of butter. Roast in a hot, 400°, oven for 45 to 50 minutes and be sure to baste every 5 minutes. Basting is important as it has to do with the flavor and juiciness of the meat. Place squab on a platter. Keep warm in a warm oven while you drain off the butter and add 1½ cups of consomme and a tablespoon of beef extract. Cook this mixture until reduced by ½, skim off excess fat, strain the gravy, pour over squab and serve garnished with watercress.

ROAST PRAIRIE CHICKEN

Procure a nice plump chicken weighing about 2½ pounds, singe, draw and wash it in cold water. Wipe with dry towel. Cut off the feet from the joint of the leg. Make an incision just under the thigh and insert the legs inside. Detach the skin as much as possible from the breast and put a layer of foremeat over the breast under the loosened skin and fill the body with the same foremeat. Sew the chicken up, truss it nicely, rub over it 1 even tablespoon of salt. Spread over it 1 even tablespoon of vegetable oil and lay a few thin slices of larding pork over the breast. Place it in a roasting pan. Add 1 cup of boiling water. Place it in a hot oven, baste frequently, and roast until done, which will take about 1 hour if the chicken is young. Place the feet, giblets and neck in a saucepan. Cover with cold water. Add 1 onion, 1 even tablespoon of salt and boil until tender. Fifteen minutes before serving, remove the boiled liver and rub it fine. Transfer the chicken to a hot dish. Take out the threads and place the chicken in a warm place. Remove the fat from the gravy. Mix ½ teaspoon of cornstarch with ½ cup of cold water. Add it to the gravy. Let it cook for a few minutes. Add sufficient giblet broth to make a creamy sauce. Strain it through a sieve. Add the fine rubbed liver and serve in a sauciere with the chicken.

FRIED PHEASANT

Preheat oven to 350°. Remove the legs and wings from a pheasant and cut the breast in half. Discard back and neck. Allow the pheasant to soak in cold water for several hours (3 tablespoons of salt to a quart of water). This is to remove any blood clots that may be in the pheasant because of shot. Remove, rinse in cold water and dry thoroughly. Place 2 slightly-beaten eggs to which has been added a tablespoon of cold water in a shallow dish. Dip pheasant in egg. Remove and roll in flour to which proper seasoning of salt and pepper has been added. Dip again in beaten egg and roll in fine dried bread crumbs. Allow to stand for an hour or two in the refrigerator, if possible. Place ½" of lard in a skillet and fry pheasant in hot fat until well browned. Brown carefully. Place fried pheasant in a covered roaster. Pour 1½ cups of cream over it and allow to steam in the covered roaster for about 40 minutes at 350° or until tender. Serve with fried bread crumbs and currant jelly.

ROAST PHEASANT

Roast only young birds - feet are still gray with rounded and flexible spurs. Salt inside of one 1 to 3 pound ready-to-cook pheasant. Stuff, if desired. Tie legs together and to tail. Place, breast up, on rack in shallow roasting pan. Lay bacon slices over breast. Roast, uncovered, at 350° for 1 to 2½ hours or until tender. Allow 1 to 1½ pounds per serving.

PHEASANT WITH APPLES

Coat two 1½ to 3 pound ready-to-cook pheasants, cut up, with mixture of ¼ cup all-purpose flour, 1 teaspoon salt and ¼ teaspoon pepper. In a skillet, lightly brown pheasant pieces in 6 tablespoons butter or margarine. Add ¾ cup sauterne. Simmer, covered, 35 to 55 minutes or until tender. Remove pheasant to serving platter. Keep warm. Reserve pan drippings. Beat ¾ cup light cream with 3 egg yolks. Slowly stir egg mixture into reserved pan drippings in skillet. Cook and stir over medium heat just until mixture is smooth and thickened. Do not boil. Pour sauce over pheasants. Garnish platter with Sauteed Apples. Makes 4 to 5 servings.

SAUTEED APPLES: In a skillet, melt 3 tablespoons butter or margarine. Add 2 apples, cored and sliced into wedges. Sprinkle with 1 teaspoon sugar. Cook apples, turning often, until lightly browned.

SMOTHERED PHEASANT

1 pheasant, whole or cut-up into pieces
1 bay leaf
Salt and pepper
1 can cream of mushroom soup
1 can cream of chicken soup
1 can cream of celery soup
⅓ C. white cooking wine or vermouth
Buttered noodles
½ C. Parmesan cheese

Place whole pheasant, breast side up, or cut-up pheasant in roaster. Salt and pepper pieces or cavity. Add bay leaf. Mix soups and wine together and pour over pheasant. Place in a small covered roaster in oven and bake for 2 hours. Serve over buttered noodles. Top with Parmesan cheese. Serves 4 easily.

ROAST WILD TURKEY

Salt and pepper inside of turkey. Fill with wild rice game stuffing. Sew up and truss. Rub the skin with a creamed mixture of 1/3 cup butter and 1/4 cup flour. Lay the bird on a dripping rack in a roasting pan. Cover the breasts with thin slices of salt pork and roast in a very hot oven (500°) for 30 minutes. When the bird is well browned, pour over it a mixture of 1/2 cup melted butter, the juice of a lemon, 1 teaspoon freshly crushed black pepper and 1 teaspoon salt. Reduce the temperature to 300° and roast the turkey slowly for 2 to 3 hours, depending upon the size of the bird. Baste every 15 minutes with the pan drippings. Thicken the pan drippings with a little browned flour and add the chopped giblets. Serve with sauce separately. Arrange the turkey on a hot platter and garnish with bouquets of crisp watercress and with apples poached in cider.

FISH & WATER LIFE

Baked Carp	75	Fried Fish Fillet	48
Baked Fish	52	Fried Soft-Shell Blue Crab	80
Baked Halibut with Cheese Sauce	66	Fried Turtle	87
Baked Stuffed Lobster	84	Frog Legs	86
Beer Batter Fish	51	Haddock Bake	62
Catfish	74	Haddock-Shrimp Bake	59
Charcoaled Salmon Steaks	78	Halibut Royale	65
Codfish Balls	58	How to Fix Bony Fish	47
Crab Casserole	81	Italian Sauced Fish	50
Crescent Cod Bake	60	Kala Mojake (Fish Chowder)	49
Crispy Coated Oven-Bake Sole	64	Mock Lobster	63
Eel, Stewed or Fried	85	Ozark Catfish Balls	73
Fillet of Sole Supreme	67	Salmon Steaks	79
Fillets Elegante	57	Scalloped Oysters	83
Fish Bake	71	Sole Mousse with Shrimp Sauce	68
Fish Chowder	77	Steamed Clams	82
Fish Fillet Baked in		Stuffed Fish	54
Wine-Mushroom Sauce	70	Stuffed Whitefish	72
Fish Fillets	56	Walleye Pike	76

HOW TO FIX BONY FISH

After fish is dressed, carve crosswise with a sharp knife. Salt to taste and roll in flour and cornmeal mixed equally. Put in hot fat and fry until brown. Put in inset pans and set in pressure cooker with ½" water in bottom of cooker. Cook for 45 minutes with 15 pounds pressure. Fish cooked this way is good warmed over in hot fat in open skillet.

FRIED FISH FILLET

2 eggs
¼ C. evaporated milk

⅓ C. beer
½ tsp. salt

Mix ingredients. Dip fish in mixture and coat evenly with Bisquick. Pop in frying pan with about 1½" of cooking oil. To keep the edges from curling, fry the fillets with outside up first. Fresh lemon and salt to taste.

KALA MOJAKE
(FISH CHOWDER)

1 onion, chopped
½ C. butter or margarine
4 C. diced raw potatoes
½ tsp. basil
2 tsp. salt
⅛ tsp. pepper
2 C. water
1 lb. frozen cod or torsk
1 C. evaporated milk

Saute onion in butter until golden. Place onion in saucepan with potatoes, spices and water. Cut fish into 2" chunks. Place on top of mixture in pan. Cover and simmer 15 minutes. Add milk. Stir gently. Cover and heat to boiling point. Serve.

ITALIAN SAUCED FISH

2-16 oz. pkgs. frozen
   flounder fillets, thawed
1-8 oz. can spaghetti sauce
   with mushrooms

2 T. chopped onion
1-4 oz. pkg. shredded
   mozzarella cheese (1 C.)

Preheat oven to 350°. Arrange fillets in single layer on well-greased baking sheet. Sprinkle with salt. Mix spaghetti sauce and onion. Pour over fillets. Bake, uncovered, at 350° until fish flakes easily with fork, about 25 to 30 minutes. Sprinkle with cheese. Return to oven until cheese melts, about 3 minutes. Use 15½x10½x1" baking sheet. Low calorie: 149 per serving. Serves 8.

BEER BATTER FISH

1 lb. fish fillets or cooked
  large shrimp or ½ lb. each
3 or 4 T. Bisquick baking mix
½ C. beer

Vegetable oil
1 egg
1 C. Bisquick baking mix
½ tsp. salt

Heat oil (1½") in heavy saucepan or deep fat frying to moderately high (350°). Lightly coat fish with 3 to 4 tablespoons baking mix. Mix 1 cup Bisquick mix, the salt, egg and beer until smooth. Dip fish into batter, letting excess batter drip into bowl. Fry until golden brown, about 7 minutes on each side. Drain. Makes 4 servings.

BAKED FISH

2 lbs. fish (flounder, cod,
    walleye, etc.)
1 tsp. salt
Ground pepper
¼ tsp. red pepper or
    ½ tsp. Tabasco
6 tsp. oil
2 large onions, sliced
2 T. pimento, diced

4 thick sliced tomatoes or 1
    can stewed (#303)
3 T. chopped chives or
    scallions
½ lb. mushrooms, sliced
¾ C. dry bread crumbs
⅓ C. dry white wine
1 tsp. Worcestershire sauce

Preheat oven to 350°. Oil pan, cover with layer of all the onions and pimento. Sprinkle Tabasco on fish and rub in. Add salt and pepper. Arrange fish on onions. Cover each fish with tomato and sprinkle with chives. Scatter mushrooms and add wine over all. Heat remaining oil in skillet. Add Worcestershire sauce and brown bread crumbs. Sprinkle over fish and bake 35 to 40 minutes. Serves 4.

NOTE: Use Tabasco liberally. Also, may want to saute onions briefly before layering.

STUFFED FISH

¼ C. chopped onion
¼ C. margarine
1-3 oz. can broiled, chopped
  mushrooms, drained
Reserved liquid from
  mushrooms
1-7½ oz. can crabmeat,
  drained
½ C. coarse cracker crumbs
2 T. parsley

½ tsp. salt
Dash of pepper
2 lbs. fish fillets
3 T. butter
3 T. flour
Milk
⅓ C. dry white wine
4 oz. shredded Swiss
  cheese (1 C.)
½ tsp. paprika

Preheat oven to 400°. In skillet, cook onion in the ¼ cup butter until tender. Take off heat, stir in mushrooms, flaked crabmeat, cracker crumbs, parsley, ½ teaspoon salt, pepper. Spread mixture over fillets, roll each fillet, place seam-side down. Add enough milk to mushroom liquid to make 1½ cups. In saucepan, melt 3 tablespoons butter and 3 tablespoons flour. Add milk mixture and cook until thick, add wine, pour over fillet rolls. Bake at 400° for 25 minutes. Sprinkle with cheese and paprika. Bake 10 minutes longer or until fish flakes easily with a fork. Serves 8.

FISH FILLETS

1 lb. frozen fish fillets
1 can cream of shrimp soup

2 to 3 T. Parmesan cheese
Butter

Place fish in buttered cookie pan. Top with soup. Sprinkle with cheese. Dot with butter. Bake at 350° for 1 hour.

FILLETS ELEGANTE

Fish fillets
Freshly ground pepper
2 T. butter or margarine

1 can frozen condensed cream of shrimp soup, thawed
¼ C. shredded Parmesan cheese
Paprika

Arrange fish fillets (sole, haddock, halibut, or cod) in buttered 9" pie plate. Dash with pepper and dot with butter or margarine. Spread shrimp soup over fillets and sprinkle with Parmesan cheese and paprika. Bake at 400° for 25 minutes. Serve with lemon wedges. Makes 4 servings.

CODFISH BALLS

½ lb. salt codfish
3 C. diced raw potatoes

1 beaten egg
2 T. butter or margarine

Freshen codfish by soaking in water several hours or overnight. Dice. Cook potatoes with codfish in boiling water until potatoes are tender. Drain. Beat with electric mixer and add egg, butter or margarine and pepper. Beat thoroughly. Drop by heaping tablespoon (about the size of golf balls) into deep hot fat (375°). Fry about 2 to 3 minutes or until golden brown, turning once. Drain. Makes 30.

HADDOCK-SHRIMP BAKE

2 lbs. frozen haddock fillets, slightly thawed
1-10½ oz. can condensed cream of potato soup
¾ C. milk
1 C. frozen, cooked shrimp
¼ C. butter, melted
½ tsp. grated onion
½ tsp. Worcestershire sauce
1¼ C. rich round cracker crumbs (30 crackers)
¼ tsp. garlic salt

Place fish in greased 13x9x2" baking dish. Heat soup and milk. Stir in shrimp. Spread over fish. Bake at 375° for 20 minutes. Combine remaining ingredients except crumbs. Mix in crumbs. Sprinkle over fish. Bake 10 minutes. Serves 6 to 8.

CRESCENT COD BAKE

4 C. water
½ lemon, quartered
1¼ to 1½ lbs. frozen,
  boneless cod fillets
1-10¾ oz. can condensed
  cream of shrimp soup

¼ C. evaporated milk or half
  and half
1-4 oz. can mushrooms,
  drained
1-8 oz. can refrigerated
  crescent rolls
¾ C. shredded Cheddar
  cheese

Preheat oven to 350°. In a large saucepan, heat water and lemon to boiling. Cut fish into 2 or 3 pieces to fit pan. Add to boiling water. Return to boiling. Reduce heat. Cover and simmer 10 minutes. Drain well. Flake fish with fork. In a medium bowl, combine soup, milk and mushrooms. Stir in flaked fish. Pour mixture into a 10" pie pan or 9" square pan. Separate dough into 8 triangles. Spoon rounded spoonful of cheese on wide end of each triangle. Fold corners over cheese and roll 2 turns. Seal ends. Arrange in a circle over fish mixture with dough points joining in the center. Bake at 350° for 30 to 40 minutes or until golden brown. Place pie pan on cookie sheet during last 10 minutes of baking to guard against spillage. Serves 8.

HADDOCK BAKE

Haddock fillets
1 tsp. salt
¼ tsp. pepper
¼ C. flour

½ C. milk
½ C. sour cream
½ C. crushed cheese
  crackers

Mix flour, salt and pepper. Coat fish on all sides. Lay fish on well-greased baking dish. Pour on milk. Bake uncovered 30 to 35 minutes at 350°, then spoon sour cream over fillets and sprinkle with cracker crumbs. Bake until done.

MOCK LOBSTER

1 lb. frozen haddock
  (or torsk)
1 qt. water

2 tsp. vinegar
1 tsp. salt
½ to 2 T. seafood seasoning

Bring water to boil. Add seasonings. Cut partially thawed haddock or torsk into strips across. Boil in water and seasonings for 15 minutes. Serve with melted lemon butter.

CRISPY COATED OVEN-BAKED SOLE

1 pkg. herb and butter
  flavor stuffing mix
2 lbs. sole fillets

¼ C. dry white wine
¼ C. butter, melted

Preheat oven to 375°. Whirl contents of seasoning packet in stuffing mix package in blender until large particles are broken up. Add stuffing crumbs and continue blending until mixture is uniform. Dry fish, dip in wine, then coat with crumbs. Arrange fish in a single layer in shallow greased pan. Bake in preheated oven for 15 minutes. Drizzle butter over fillets and return to oven 5 minutes longer. Serves 5 to 6.

NOTE: Use leftover crumbs another time to coat fish, veal, scallops or chicken breasts.

HALIBUT ROYALE

In shallow dish, combine 3 tablespoons lemon juice, 1 teaspoon salt and ½ teaspoon paprika. Add 6 halibut steaks and marinate for 1 hour, turning steaks after 30 minutes. Cook ½ cup chopped onion in 2 tablespoons butter until tender, but not brown. Place steaks in greased 10x6x1½" baking dish. Top with 6 green pepper strips and sprinkle with onion. Bake at 450° about 10 minutes. Serves 6.

BAKED HALIBUT WITH CHEESE SAUCE

2½ lbs. halibut steaks,
  1" thick
3 T. butter
4 T. flour
1⅛ tsp. salt

Pepper
¼ tsp. nutmeg
1½ C. milk
¾ C. grated American
  cheese
Paprika

Wipe fish with damp cloth. Remove skin and bones. Place in well-greased baking dish. Sprinkle with a little salt and pepper. Melt butter in a saucepan. Add flour, salt, pepper and nutmeg and stir until smooth. Add milk slowly and cook until thickened and smooth. Stir in cheese until melted. Pour sauce over fish. Sprinkle with paprika and bake at 325° for 45 minutes. Serves 4 to 6.

FILLET OF SOLE SUPREME

3½ T. butter or oleo
1 T. flour
½ tsp. salt
2 tsp. lemon juice
¼ tsp. prepared horseradish
⅛ tsp. monosodium glutamate
Dash of pepper
⅓ C. milk
1-7½ oz. can crabmeat, boned and flaked
4 sole or flounder fillets
Paprika
1 pkg. frozen lima beans

Preheat oven to 350°. Make sauce, adding seasonings and add crabmeat. Mix well. Arrange 2 fillets in shallow baking dish. Spread with ½ crab mixture. Top with remaining crab mixture. Brush with remaining butter and lemon juice. Arrange beans around fish. Bake for 25 to 30 minutes. Makes 4 servings.

SOLE MOUSSE WITH SHRIMP SAUCE

1 lb. fillet of sole
2 C. heavy cream
4 eggs
⅔ C. milk
1 tsp. parsley flakes
1½ tsp. salt

¼ tsp. savory
⅛ tsp. white pepper
Dash cayenne
1 T. butter
1 T. fine dry bread crumbs
¼ tsp. dill weed

Cut sole in small pieces. Place ½ cup cream in blender jar. Add ¼ of the fish and blend at medium speed until smooth. Add 1 whole egg. Scrape down sides of jar with rubber spatula and blend again until smooth. Mixture will become very thick. Turn out into a bowl and repeat until all of the fish is blended with all of the cream. Stir milk, parsley, salt, savory, white pepper and cayenne into fish mixture, blending well. Spread all the butter in a 6-cup mold. Combine bread crumbs and dill. Sprinkle over bottom and sides of mold. Spoon fish mixture into mold; level top with spatula. Set in pan of hot water. Bake in 350° oven for 45 minutes until top is lightly browned and knife inserted in center comes out clean. Let stand 15 minutes before removing from mold. Serve with Shrimp Sauce. Serves 6.

SHRIMP SAUCE:
¼ C. butter
3 T. flour
1½ C. half and half
½ tsp. salt
½ tsp. onion powder
3 T. dry sherry
1 T. lemon juice
2 tsp. parsley flakes
2 C. cooked and cleaned shrimp

Melt butter. Stir in flour. Add half and half, salt and onion powder. Cook, stirring until sauce boils and thickens. Stir in sherry, lemon juice and parsley flakes. Add shrimp and heat through. Makes 3 cups of sauce.

FISH FILLET BAKED IN
WINE-MUSHROOM SAUCE

1 to 1⅓ lbs. fish fillets
  (sole or halibut)
3 T. butter or margarine
3 T. flour

1 can cream of mushroom
  soup
½ C. white wine
2 T. Parmesan cheese,
  grated
2 T. parsley, chopped

Melt butter. Stir in flour. Add soup and wine and cook, stirring constantly until mixture boils and thickens. Add cheese and parsley. Arrange fish in single layer in shallow, greased baking dish. Pour sauce over fish. Bake at 375° for 25 minutes or until fish flakes. Serves 3 to 4.

FISH BAKE

2 lbs. flounder
3 tomatoes, cubed
1 medium onion, cubed
½ C. sliced olives
¼ C. margarine
¼ C. soy sauce
⅛ C. lemon juice
Salt and pepper to taste

Place fish in foil in 9x13" baking dish. Layer vegetables on top. Pour over melted butter and other sauces. Wrap tightly in foil. Bake at 350° for 1 hour. Serves 6 to 8.

STUFFED WHITEFISH

1-3 lb. dressed whitefish
  or other fish, boned
¼ C. chopped onion
3 T. chopped green pepper
1 T. butter

1-12 oz. can whole kernel
  corn, drained
1 C. soft bread crumbs
2 T. chopped canned
  pimento
⅛ tsp. dried thyme, crushed
2 T. salad oil

Sprinkle inside of fish with salt. Place in well-greased shallow pan. Cook onion and pepper in butter. Stir in next 4 ingredients and ½ teaspoon salt. Stuff fish loosely. Brush with oil. Cover with foil. Bake at 350° for 45 to 60 minutes. Serves 6.

OZARK CATFISH BALLS

Bake or steam catfish. (Modern method is to cook in a pressure cooker.) Remove fish from bones and flake. To every 2 cups flaked fish, add 2 cups mashed potatoes, 1 egg, salt and pepper to taste. Shape in balls and fry in deep fat.

CATFISH SOUP

2 to 3 lbs. catfish, cut up
2 qts. cold water
1 sliced onion
1 chopped celery stalk

Salt and pepper
Herbs (bay leaf, parsley,
 thyme)
1 C. milk
2 T. butter or fat

Place all ingredients into stewpan and put on slow fire. Stir occasionally and cook until fish is ready to fall to pieces. Serve hot.

BAKED CARP

Choose fresh, clear, cold water carp and skin the same as catfish. Cut up as if to fry. Choose size of roaster to suit amount of fish, then put in a layer of fish, rolled in flour with salt and pepper. Then add a layer of bacon strips, then another layer of fish, etc., topping with a layer of smoked bacon strips. Bake and serve warm.

WALLEYE PIKE

1⅓ C. butter
5 C. soft bread crumbs
¼ C. onion
Pinch of dill

Juice of ¼ lemon
1 clove garlic
Salt
8 large fillets

Soften butter and add rest of ingredients. Spread over fillets in large pan. Bake at 350° for 15 to 20 minutes or until browned.

FISH CHOWDER

2 lbs. fresh lake trout (salmon or cod)
¼ lb. diced salt pork or bacon
1 C. finely chopped onion
2 tsp. salt (more or less)
2 tsp. pepper (more or less)
1 small bay leaf
5 medium potatoes, diced
2 qts. milk
2 medium carrots, diced
2 C. celery, diced

Clean and fillet fish. Cut into small pieces. Dice the salt pork or bacon and fry slowly in heavy skillet until crisp and brown. Meanwhile, cook potatoes and carrots but do not drain. Combine the cooked salt pork and cooked vegetables. In the fat, cook the onions and celery. Add to others. Next, add the fish and milk and simmer until fish is tender. Do not boil. Yield: 3½ quarts.

CHARCOALED SALMON STEAKS

2 salmon steaks (or 2 pike
   or bass fillets)
¼ C. butter
1 T. lemon juice

1½ tsp. snipped parsley or
   dry parsley flakes
¼ tsp. grated lemon rind

Heat butter, lemon juice, rind and parsley in saucepan. Blend. Arrange fish
in long-handled hinged broiler. Brush generously with basting sauce. Place
broiler over hot coals and boil 5 minutes on each side until lightly crisped,
using any remaining sauce while broiling.

SALMON STEAKS

Place 4 salmon steaks, 1" thick, in shallow baking pan. Blend ⅓ cup melted butter, 1 teaspoon Worcestershire sauce, 1 teaspoon grated onion and ¼ teaspoon paprika. Brush some lightly on fish. Sprinkle with salt. Bake at 350° for 25 to 30 minutes. Pass remaining sauce. Serves 4.

FRIED SOFT-SHELL BLUE CRAB

Sprinkle 8 cleaned soft-shell blue crabs with salt. Roll in a mixture of ½ cup fine saltine cracker crumbs and 1 tablespoon all-purpose flour. Dip in mixture of 1 slightly-beaten egg and ½ cup milk. Roll in crumbs and flour again. Heat a small amount of salad oil in a skillet. Fry crabs in hot fat 3 to 5 minutes on each side, depending on size of crabs. Drain. Serves 4.

TO DEEP-FAT FRY: Fry coated crabs in deep, hot fat, 350°, 4 minutes or until golden. Drain thoroughly on paper toweling.

CRAB CASSEROLE

1 lb. crabmeat
2 T. melted butter
2 hard-boiled eggs
1 tsp. minced onion
2 tsp. minced parsley

1 pt. light cream
2 T. catsup
2 T. bread crumbs
1 tsp. lemon juice
Paprika

Preheat oven to 350°. Soften onions in a little butter. Don't brown. Add the rest of the ingredients. Put in a shallow casserole with bread crumbs on top. Sprinkle with paprika before serving. Bake ½ hour. Serves 4.

STEAMED CLAMS

Thoroughly wash 5 dozen soft-shelled clams in shells (oval shape). Cover with salt water ($\frac{1}{3}$ cup to 1 gallon cold water). Let stand 15 minutes. Rinse. Repeat twice. Place clams on rack in kettle with 1 cup hot water. Cover tightly and steam just until shells open, about 5 minutes. Cut out and serve on half shell with melted butter. Makes 4 servings.

SCALLOPED OYSTERS

1 pt. oysters
2 C. medium-coarse cracker crumbs (46 crackers)
½ C. butter, melted
¾ C. light cream
½ tsp. salt
¼ tsp. Worcestershire sauce

Drain oysters, reserving ¼ cup liqueur. Combine crumbs and butter. Spread a third of crumbs in 8x1½" round pan. Cover with half the oysters. Sprinkle with pepper. Using another third of the crumbs, spread a second layer; cover with remaining oysters. Sprinkle with pepper. Bake in moderate oven (350°) for 40 minutes.

BAKED STUFFED LOBSTER

Preheat oven to 450°. Prepare a live lobster by splitting and removing the stomach and entrail. Reserve the red roe and also the green liver of the lobster. Saute the red roe and green liver in a little melted butter. Add 1 teaspoon finely grated onion or onion juice. Add 1 teaspoon finely minced parsley. Season with salt, pepper and thyme. Add some finely crushed or rolled cracker crumbs in sufficient quantity to fill the cavity. Bake in a 400° oven for 12 to 15 minutes. We recommend using a small to medium-sized lobster for this dish and serving a whole lobster for each individual. During cooking period, baste slightly with melted butter so that the lobster will not dry out. Serve with lemon slices.

EEL
(STEWED OR FRIED)

Skin and clean the eels, cut off their heads and take out all that is stringy. Cut into pieces about 3" long. Parboil them about 10 minutes, drain off water, then put on one pint of veal or similar soup stock. Season with salt, butter and pepper. Boil slowly about 25 minutes, then thicken with flour and pour over them. Use parsley or onion if you like. Fry eels the same as fish, after parboiling.

FROG LEGS

Skin the frog legs, wash and cut off feet. Soak at least 1 hour in salt water. Lightly beat egg. Season legs with salt and pepper. Dip in cornmeal (or bread crumbs), then in egg and again in cornmeal. Fry in deep hot fat. Drain fat before serving.

FRIED TURTLE

To fry turtle, it is advised to parboil or cook in pressure cooker until tender first. Then roll in flour or meal and seasonings. Fry in deep fat.

NOTES • NOTES • NOTES • NOTES • NOTES

SMALL GAME

Baked Possum	103	
Chicken-Fried Coon	102	
Coon and Dressing	101	
Creamed Sour Rabbit	96	
Fried Rabbit	89	
Fried Squirrel	98	
German Style Hasenpfeffer	95	
Ground Hog	106	
How to Cook a Coon	100	
Marsh Rabbit	94	
Porcupine	107	
Possum & Chestnuts	105	
Possum	104	
Rabbit Hunter's Style	92	
Raccoon Preparation	99	
Squirrel Preparation	97	
Stewed Rabbit	90	

FRIED RABBIT

1 C. flour
1 tsp. salt
Pepper to taste

Cooking fat
1 C. diced onion
Juice of ¼ lemon

Cut rabbit up in pieces desired. Roll pieces in mixture of flour, salt and pepper. Brown the rabbit in at least 4 tablespoons cooking fat and then add diced onions and lemon juice. Cover and cook until done.

STEWED RABBIT

1 pair of rabbits
1 glass Claret wine
2 onions
1 sq. inch of ham
3 T. vegetable oil

1 clove garlic, chopped very
  fine
1 herb bouquet, chopped
  fine
1 C. water
1 small can mushrooms

Stewed rabbit is a great dish among the Creoles. They say that this is the only way to cook a rabbit. Proceed as follows: Skin and clean the rabbit. Wash well and cut into pieces at the joints and rub well with salt and pepper. Chop 2 onions very fine and put them in the stewpan with 3 tablespoons of vegetable oil. Let them brown slightly. Then add the rabbit and let it brown slightly. Then add 1 teaspoon of flour and let this brown a little. Chop the square inch of ham very fine, mincing it, and add. Then add the clove of garlic and 2 sprigs each of thyme and parsley and 1 bay leaf, minced fine. Let this brown nicely and pour over 1 glass of good Claret wine. Let this cook 10 minutes, stirring it constantly. Then add 1 cup of boiling water. Stir well, season again to taste and let it boil for 30 minutes and serve hot. Green peas or potatoes, boiled or mashed, make a nice entree for this dish.

RABBIT
(HUNTER'S STYLE)

A pair of rabbits
3 T. vegetable oil
1 onion
1 slice of ham
1 T. flour
1 clove garlic
2 sprigs thyme

2 bay leaves
½ box mushrooms
Zest of 1 lemon
½ bottle Claret wine
Salt and pepper to taste
Croutons to garnish

Prepare the rabbit, clean and draw, and cut into pieces at the joints. Rub well with salt and pepper. Put 3 tablespoons of vegetable oil into the saucepan with the rabbit and let it brown slowly. When nearly brown, add the onion, chopped fine, and let this brown slightly. Then add the ham, minced very fine and the clove of garlic and bay leaves and thyme, minced very fine. Stir with the rabbit, and let these brown for about 2 minutes. Then add a tablespoon of flour and brown for a few minutes. Add ½ bottle of Claret wine and let all cook for about 1 hour. Season according to taste. Add ½ can of mushrooms, chopped fine, and the zest of a lemon and again season to taste. Let all cook for 30 minutes longer and serve on a hot dish with croutons fried in butter.

MARSH RABBIT

8 or 10 muskrat saddles

Soak in cold water 3 to 5 days. Change water every day until saddles are white. Cook until tender. Drain water off and place in pan. Pour barbeque sauce over meat and bake ½ hour in preheated 350° oven. Very delicious. Serves 8 to 10.

GERMAN STYLE HASENPFEFFER

Clean the hare or rabbit well. Cut into small pieces. Put in a saucepan 2 tablespoons of vegetable oil. When hot, add chopped fine 1 bay leaf, 1 clove, 1 clove garlic, 2 tablespoons of diced bacon, 2 small carrots, chopped fine and a few mushrooms. Put in the cut-up hare and when well browned, pour over it ½ cup of vinegar together with 1½ cups of water. Cover and simmer until tender. Just before removing from the fire, add 1 cup of cream and serve hot in a border of noodles. This is a very delicious delicacy.

CREAMED SOUR RABBIT

Cut rabbit in small pieces and soak overnight in a solution of 1 cup vinegar and ½ cup water. Next morning, cook rabbit in the vinegar solution until done. Thicken the broth with a little flour. Salt and pepper to taste. Serve hot. Good with biscuits.

SQUIRREL PREPARATION

Squirrels are skinned by using a sharp knife, cutting around the rear legs at the knee, cutting down from one side, around the vent and to the other, starting the skin, and peeling out the squirrel, drawing the hide over the head. Cut the squirrel in 5 serving portions, 4 quarters and the one piece of back. Look for the small waxy scent glands inside the forelegs. Remove them. Parboil in water with soda for 15 minutes to remove the over-strong flavor. You can use squirrel for any rabbit dish.

FRIED SQUIRREL

Dress squirrel. Wash thoroughly. Cut in pieces for servings. Cover with salted water. Let stand overnight. Drain. If squirrel is not tender, parboil 10 minutes. Drain. Roll in flour. Fry in vegetable oil until tender. If the squirrel is young, parboiling is unnecessary. Make a brown sauce. Serve squirrel garnished with lemon slices and parsley.

RACCOON PREPARATION

In preparing a raccoon for cooking, clean thoroughly inside and out after the pelt has been removed. When the pelt is prime, the meat is also good. Be sure to remove the kernel-shaped glands in the muscles of the armpits and between the legs. You will have to cut into the meat a little to extract these. Coon, like possum, is only good during winter months.

HOW TO COOK A COON

Cut up coon and boil in water and let stand overnight. Take out of water next morning and wash 2 times and put in kettle and boil until tender. Put in a bread pan and put pepper and sage on it and bake. Serve with sweet potatoes.

COON AND DRESSING

Cut coon into small pieces and salt to taste. Cook in the inset pan of the pressure cooker for about an hour at 15 pounds pressure. Cook longer if it is an old tough coon. When coon is tender, arrange pieces in a baking dish and cover with dressing made as follows: Moisten 8 to 10 slices of dry bread with the juice cooked from the coon and add 2 eggs, 2 tablespoons sage, ½ teaspoon ground cloves, and 1 tablespoon salt. Bake in oven at 350° until the dressing is browned. This assures a tender, tasty coon without being too fat and greasy. Also good for possum

CHICKEN-FRIED COON

Use only a small animal. Cut in small pieces for frying. Soak these in milk to cover for 40 minutes. Remove, roll in flour, well seasoned with salt and pepper and fry in deep fat. Gravy can be made by pouring off most of the fat, leaving just enough to cover the bottom of the pan. Stir in seasoned flour, brown and use the milk in which the meat of the coon was soaked for liquid in the gravy.

BAKED POSSUM

Possum is a traditional Southern dish. If the possum is to be used for meat and not the skin, dip the whole animal in boiling water as farmers do a freshly killed pig. Scrape the hair off, leaving the skin on. Dress the possum. Boil to doneness in water with pepper and salt as for coon. Remove when done, place in a baking dish, season with black pepper, sprinkle with flour, put sweet potatoes around the roast, add bay leaves on the roast, if you wish, and brown to crispness. If the roasting is done slowly, over a long period, there will be a tendency to render out much of the fat that sometimes makes a possum a rather greasy dish. Possum may also be barbecued, using the same recipe as for coon. Possum is only good during winter months.

POSSUM

Take a possum and parboil until tender. Take out of water and put in bread pan, then pepper to taste. Take 3 large sweet potatoes and boil until tender. Lay these around possum in bread pan. Put in oven and bake until brown. Serve warm.

POSSUM AND CHESTNUTS

Skin possum, remove glands and entrails. Scrape clean and scald in boiling water. Rub inside and out with salt and pepper and set in cool place. Stuff with chestnuts, applesauce, and bread crumbs in equal portions. Cover with slices of sweet potato, 1 cup boiling water, ½ cup lemon juice. Bake in butter and baste often until tender.

GROUND HOG

When ground hog is dressed, be sure to move the kernel from under the front legs to keep from making it taste. Cut up and salt to taste. Roll in flour. Put in hot fat and fry until brown. Then put in inset pans in pressure cooker with ½" water in bottom of cooker. Cook for 70 minutes with 15 pounds pressure. Possum can be cooked the same way with good results.

PORCUPINE

Dress porcupine. It is easily done. There are no quills on the belly and the skin peels as freely as a rabbit's. Take him to camp, parboil him for 30 minutes and roast or broil him to a rich brown over a bed of glowing coals. He will need no pork to make him juicy, and you will find him very much like spring lamb, only better. It may be either roasted or made into a stew in the manner of hares, but must be parboiled at least half an hour to be tender. One part of the porcupine is always a delicacy, the liver, which is easily removed by making a cut just under the neck into which hand is thrust, and the liver pulled out. It may be fried with bacon, or baked slowly and carefully in the baker-pan with slices of bacon.

NOTES • NOTES • NOTES • NOTES • NOTES

LARGE GAME

Barbecued Venison Ribs 121	Moose Steak (Northern Style) 127
Bear Steak 129	Pot Roast of Venison 123
Boiled Venison Steaks 115	Roast Venison (A German Recipe) 126
Canadian Rockies Bison or	Roast Venison 113
Buffalo Pot Roast 130	To Lard Game 109
Correct Procedure with Your Deer,	Venison 114
Antelope, Elk or Moose Meat 110	Venison Jerky 117
Deer Liver 112	Venison Meatballs 118
Deer Steaks 116	Venison Stew 119
Hawaiian Venison 120	Venison Swiss Steak 122
Moose Steak (Cowboy Style) 128	Venison, Hunter's Style 124

TO LARD GAME

Larding fat is used for venison, other game, certain cuts of meat and poultry. Larding pork is salt pork which must be white and firm, and kept perfectly dry and cold, especially in warm weather. Its hardness makes it easier to cut evenly. It is quite desirable to have a regular larding fork or needle to lard meat. These chunks of larding pork or lardons, as they are called, should be cut in strips from 3 to 3½" long and from ¼ to ½" wide, depending on the size and pieces of meat to be larded.

CORRECT PROCEDURE WITH YOUR DEER, ANTELOPE, ELK OR MOOSE MEAT

The man who comes home from a successful big game hunt generally has a problem as to how to handle several hundred pounds of meat. First, the animal should be thoroughly cleaned, and then allows to age from one to four weeks at a temperature of around 35°. Get a butcher to cut it up, as he would veal or beef, into chops, steaks, roasts and stew meat. Have him trim off all fats, since the fat or tallow of these animals is strong. It is much like mutton fat and is inclined to stick to the roof of the mouth when cooked with the meat. As an extra precaution, be sure the meat is sweet and clean, and not sour through previous mishandling. Be sure that all bruised, shot-up, or bloody sections of meat are trimmed out. In cooking, use salt pork strips or salt pork rendered fat to replace the fat removed from the animal.

Freezing the meat will not make it more tender, unless it has been aged previous to freezing or canning. We recommend that all roast from older animals be pot-roasted to keep them from becoming too dry. Steaks or chops can be broiled and pan-fried. Round steaks can be cut as Swiss steak or like a Spanish steak with onions, tomatoes and mushrooms. Pan-fried or broiled steaks or chops should be cooked rare or medium rare; otherwise, they will be tough and dry.

DEER LIVER

Wash your deer liver carefully and soak in salted water. Prepare in thin slices as you would calves liver. Season with salt and pepper. Dust with flour. Fry as many strips of bacon as you wish. Remove the bacon and hold in warming oven. Place your strips of deer liver in the bacon grease and fry until cooked to the consistency that you wish. Some people like liver well done, but well-done liver is always hard and tough. A variation to the above can be had by slicing some onions in very thin slices and browning them in a little butter and placing the fried onions on top of the liver when it is served.

ROAST VENISON

Wipe venison with cloth soaked in vinegar. Never use water as it toughens meat fibers. Dredge with flour, already salted and peppered. Place strips of bacon on meat fastened with toothpicks. (This will provide the lard.) Slice onion into rings and throw rings over (3 to each strip). Start in a brisk oven. Reduce heat and bake slowly. Three-fourths of an hour before serving, pour tomato soup (not creamed) over meat. This makes a most delicious Spanish sauce or gravy. For a 6 to 8 pound roast, use 2 cups tomato soup.

Time in oven varies according to the age of the deer.

VENISON STEAK

Venison steaks are treated like beefsteak. They are cut three-quarters of an inch thick and broiled or fried. They may be served plain with hot vegetable oil, pepper and salt or a brown gravy, but most people prefer a currant jelly sauce or having currant or wild plum jelly served with each portion. For roasting venison, the saddle or leg will be found best. Cook 10 minutes to the pound, treating it the same as mutton. Make a good brown gravy from the drippings left in the pan and stock made from the trimmings of the roast and serve very hot with currant, wild plum or barberry jelly.

BOILED VENISON STEAKS

Brush 4-½" thick venison steaks from leg, rib or loin chops of young animal with 2 tablespoons salad oil. Let stand 15 minutes. Broil steaks 3" from heat for 7 to 10 minutes; turn. Broil on other side for 7 to 10 minutes. Combine ¼ cup melted butter or margarine, 1 tablespoon onion juice, and dash of salt. Brush on broiled steaks. Makes 4 servings.

DEER STEAKS

1½ lbs. deer steak
  (1½" thick)
2 large onions
2 T. fat

1½ C. water
Salt
Pepper
Flour

Beat steaks with back of butcher knife to tenderize. Dip into salt-pepper-flour mixture and fry in 2 tablespoons fat over medium-hot burner. Slice onions thinly over steaks and pour in 1½ cups water. Cover and simmer for 20 minutes.

VENISON JERKY

5 lbs. ground venison
16 tsp. salt
2 tsp. black pepper
1 tsp. red cayenne pepper
1½ tsp. Tender Quick
1½ tsp. cardamon
1 tsp. marjoram
3 tsp. Accent
2 tsp. garlic powder

Mix spices with ground venison. Press meat between sheets of tin foil or wax paper. Get as thin as possible. Mix 1 ounce of liquid smoke with 1 ounce water and brush onto meat. Drape meat on racks in oven. Remove paper. Bake at 160° for 3 to 4 hours. When meat is dry, cut in strips.

VENISON MEATBALLS

3 lbs. ground venison
1 lb. pork sausage
2 C. bread crumbs
2 eggs

1 C. milk
1 C. chopped onion
Dash salt
Dash pepper

Preheat oven to 350°. Thoroughly mix venison and pork sausage. Combine other ingredients and mix with meats thoroughly. Roll into bite-size meatballs. Bake for approximately 30 to 45 minutes on cookie sheet at 350°. Serve as appetizer or main dish. Makes approximately 100 meatballs. Serve with onion gravy that has 3 ounces of blackberry wine added to it.

VENISON STEW

1½ lbs. venison, cubed
⅓ C. flour
1½ C. Burgundy wine
1-8 oz. can whole small onions
1 C. defrosted frozen peas
½ C. sour cream
½ pkg. pie crust mix
1 tsp. cornstarch
2 T. shortening
¼ tsp. pepper
1 tsp. dry mustard
½ tsp. paprika
1½ tsp. salt

Mix dry ingredients and dredge meat in same. Brown slowly in hot shortening. Add wine and bring to a boil. Turn into 9" square baking dish. Cover with foil and bake 1½ to 2 hours at 300° or until venison is very tender. Stir cornstarch into sour cream. Add drained onions and peas. Slowly stir into meat. Prepare pastry according to box. Roll to fit dish. Flute edges and slash to let steam escape. Bake in 400° oven about 20 minutes or until browned. Serves 4 to 6.

HAWAIIAN VENISON

1 lb. venison steaks
¼ C. flour
¼ C. butter
½ C. boiling water

1 tsp. salt
2 to 3 green peppers
½ C. pineapple chunks

Cut steaks in 1" cubes. Flour and brown in hot fat. Add water and salt. Simmer until tender. Clean peppers. Cut in 1" squares and boil 10 minutes. Drain. Add pineapple and pepper to meat. Pour Hawaiian Sauce over meat mixture and simmer 5 minutes. Serve over crisp Chinese noodles and/or rice.

BARBECUED VENISON RIBS

3 to 4 lbs. venison ribs
1 medium onion

½ C. barbecue sauce
1-10½ oz. can tomato soup

Preheat oven to 350°. Roll the venison ribs in flour and brown them in a frying pan on the top of the stove. Then put the ribs in a Dutch oven and slice a medium-size onion on it. Salt and pepper them. Pour ½ cup of barbecue sauce over them. Now take a can of tomato soup and pour it into the Dutch oven over the ribs. Stir the barbecue sauce and tomato soup to mix them up with the ribs. Cover it and bake 3 hours. Serves 4 to 5.

VENISON SWISS STEAK

2 lbs. venison round steak
8 medium potatoes
2-8 oz. cans tomato sauce
1½ C. frozen corn

1 small onion
Garlic salt
Salt
Pepper

Season steak lightly with garlic salt, salt and pepper. Place steak, tomato sauce and diced onion in slow cooker. Cook on medium heat for 3 hours. Add 8 potatoes, cut in half and 1 cup frozen corn. Cook an additional 1½ hours on low to medium heat. Serves 6.

POT ROAST OF VENISON

Trim carefully and remove all surplus fibers, skin and fat from either the haunch or loin of venison. Prepare and lard with salt pork lardons. Add 2 or 3 medium-sized onions, 4 carrots, 2 turnips, if available, some parsley, several stalks of celery, pinch of rosemary, thyme 2 bay leaves, 2 strips of lemon peel, salt, 8 peppercorns, dry red wine and sour cream. Put the sliced vegetables and finely chopped herbs in a Dutch oven and add equal parts of red wine and water. Bring to a boil and simmer for about 2 hours. Then remove the venison from the Dutch oven, which has been well-rinsed out or place in a roasting pan and pour the liquid over it, adding ½ cup sour cream and cook slowly until well done. Serve with potato balls and red currant jelly.

VENISON
(HUNTER'S STYLE)

3 lbs. venison meat
2 T. butter
1 onion
1 sq. inch of ham
1 T. flour
1 clove garlic
2 sprigs thyme

2 bay leaves
½ box mushrooms
Zest of 1 lemon
1 glass white wine
Salt and pepper to taste
Croutons to garnish

Cut the venison into pieces of about 2" square. Salt and pepper well. Put 2 tablespoons of vegetable oil into a saucepan with the venison and let it brown slowly. When nearly brown, add 1 onion, chopped fine and let this brown slightly. Then add the ham, minced very fine and the clove of garlic and bay leaves and thyme, minced very fine. Stir in with the venison and let these brown for about 2 minutes. Then add a tablespoon of flour and let it simmer for 5 minutes more. Then add a quart of consomme or water and let all cook for about 1 hour. Season again according to taste and add ½ can of mushrooms, chopped fine, and the rest of a lemon and season again to taste. Let all cook ½ hour longer and serve on a hot dish with croutons fried in vegetable oil.

ROAST VENISON
(GERMAN STYLE)

Wash and wipe the venison, then beat it well. Flay off the skin. Take bacon strips rather more than 2" long and lard all over the fleshy parts. Roast the meat, basting constantly. Use sour cream or butter and milk for the purpose. Send to table with a sauce made by adding water to the bastings, skimming and straining and adding pepper, salt and lemon juice.

MOOSE STEAK
(NORTHERN STYLE)

Rub moose steaks with vegetable oil or marinate in French dressing. They may be boiled slowly, turning frequently, or pan-broiled or pan-fried in a small amount of fat, using butter and meat drippings. A longer time should be allowed for the cooking than for a beefsteak. For a moose roast, it is well to cut the meat in individual servings. Sear the pieces of meat in hot vegetable oil. Season with salt and pepper. Add a small amount of boiling water. Cook slowly as a pot roast or in a slow oven, 350°, until tender. Allow a longer time than for cooking beef.

MOOSE STEAK
(COWBOY STYLE)

Cut a thick steak from the rump of a young moose. With a sharp knife, make an incision in the shape of a cross and fill it with shredded horseradish. Dip steak in oil and fry or broil quickly, turning twice, Serve with fried onions and a deviled sauce with jelly.

BEAR STEAK

Steak cut from younger bear is very good and tastes almost like beefsteak. Dust with salt and broil or fry in vegetable oil like beefsteak. Serve with anchovy, mustard or other sharp sauces. Bear tongue is prepared the same as mutton tongue.

CANADIAN ROCKIES BISON
OR BUFFALO POT ROAST

Pare and lard a haunch (6 pounds) from the rump of a young buffalo. Put in a jar and pour a marinade over it. Let stand for 24 hours, then wipe dry and save marinade. Brown meat for 20 minutes over a fast fire. Sprinkle with 2 spoons of flour and moisten with stock to cover. Add the marinade and 1 spoon of tomato puree and cook until tender, about 1 hour. Skim off the fat. Remove meat. Slice it and arrange on deep platter. Strain the gravy and thicken, if necessary. Pour some of it over the meat and serve some on the side. Serve with sweet potatoes glazed in maple syrup.

UNI-Cookbook Categories

1100	Cookies	3400	Low Cholesterol
1200	Casseroles	3500	Chocoholic
1300	Meat Dishes	3700	Cajun
1400	Microwave	3800	Household Hints
1500	Cooking for "2"	3900	Incredible Candy
1600	Slow Cooking	6100	Chinese Recipes
1700	Low Calorie	6400	German Recipes
1900	Pastries & Pies	6700	Italian Recipes
2000	Outdoor Grilling	6800	Irish Recipes
2100	Appetizers	7000	Mexican Recipes
2200	Beef	7100	Norwegian Recipes
2300	Holiday Collections	7200	Swedish Recipes
2400	Salads & Dressings		
2500	How to Cook Wild Game		
2600	Soups		
3100	Seafood & Fish		
3200	Poultry		
3300	My Own Recipes		

Available Titles 1/95

Titles change

G & R
Publishing Co.
507 Industrial Street
Waverly, IA 50677